SHIT HAPPENS GET OVER IT

summersdale

SHIT HAPPENS GET OVER IT

First published in 2011
This edition copyright © Summersdale Publishers Ltd, 2017

An Hachette UK Company
www.hachette.co.uk

Summersdale Publishers Ltd
Part of Octopus Publishing Group Limited
Carmelite House
50 Victoria Embankment
LONDON
EC4Y 0DZ
UK

www.summersdale.com

Printed and bound in Croatia

ISBN: 978-1-78685-021-8

Substantial discounts on bulk quantities of Summersdale books are available to corporations, professional associations and other organisations. For details contact general enquiries: telephone: +44 (0) 1243 771107 or email: enquiries@summersdale.com.

To. **Debbie !**

From. **Santa x**

IF YOU
ARE GOING
THROUGH
HELL,
KEEP GOING.

Winston Churchill

TO SUCCEED IN LIFE, YOU NEED THREE THINGS: A WISHBONE, A BACKBONE AND A FUNNY BONE.

Reba McEntire

LET LIFE
HAPPEN
TO YOU.
BELIEVE ME:
LIFE IS IN
THE RIGHT,
ALWAYS.

Rainer Maria Rilke

NOBODY CAN GO
BACK AND START
A NEW BEGINNING,
BUT ANYONE CAN
START TODAY
AND MAKE A
NEW ENDING.

Maria Robinson

WHAT'S DONE IS DONE.

William Shakespeare

GENIUS
IS DIVINE
PERSEVERANCE.

Woodrow Wilson

IF YOU CAN FIND
A PATH WITH
NO OBSTACLES,
IT PROBABLY
DOESN'T LEAD
ANYWHERE.

Frank A. Clark

DON'T GO AROUND SAYING THE WORLD OWES YOU A LIVING. THE WORLD OWES YOU NOTHING. IT WAS HERE FIRST.

Mark Twain

SOMETIMES YOU
JUST HAVE TO PEE
IN THE SINK.

Charles Bukowski

A KICK IN THE PANTS CAN BE THE BEST THING IN THE WORLD FOR YOU.

Walt Disney

SOME DAYS
YOU'RE
THE BUG.
SOME DAYS
YOU'RE THE
WINDSHIELD.

Price Cobb

YOU CAN'T
BE BRAVE IF
YOU'VE ONLY
HAD WONDERFUL
THINGS HAPPEN
TO YOU.

Mary Tyler Moore

LIFE: IT IS ABOUT THE GIFT, NOT THE PACKAGE IT COMES IN.

Dennis P. Costea Jr

IF WE HAD NO
WINTER, THE
SPRING WOULD
NOT BE SO
PLEASANT: IF
WE DID NOT
SOMETIMES TASTE
OF ADVERSITY,
PROSPERITY
WOULD NOT BE
SO WELCOME.

Anne Bradstreet

SOMETIMES YOU CAN GET A SPLINTER EVEN SLIDING DOWN A RAINBOW.

Cherralea Morgen

NEVER COMPLAIN AND NEVER EXPLAIN.

Benjamin Disraeli

STAND UP AND WALK OUT OF YOUR HISTORY.

Phil McGraw

IF YOU ONLY
DO WHAT
YOU KNOW
YOU CAN DO
– YOU NEVER
DO VERY
MUCH.

Tom Krause

ACCEPT THE
IMPOSSIBLE, DO
WITHOUT THE
INDISPENSABLE
AND BEAR THE
INTOLERABLE.

Kathleen Norris

ANYONE WHO TRADES LIBERTY FOR SECURITY DESERVES NEITHER.

Benjamin Franklin

DO NOT
SPOIL WHAT
YOU HAVE
BY DESIRING
WHAT YOU
HAVE NOT.

Epicurus

PEOPLE HAVE TO REALLY SUFFER BEFORE THEY CAN RISK DOING WHAT THEY LOVE.

Chuck Palahniuk

PERSEVERANCE IS FAILING NINETEEN TIMES AND SUCCEEDING THE TWENTIETH.

Julie Andrews

LIVE TODAY, FOR
TOMORROW IT
WILL ALL BE
HISTORY.

Proverb

THERE ARE DAYS WHEN IT TAKES ALL YOU'VE GOT JUST TO KEEP UP WITH THE LOSERS.

Robert Orben

LIFE ONLY DEMANDS FROM YOU THE STRENGTH THAT YOU POSSESS. ONLY ONE FEAT IS POSSIBLE – NOT TO RUN AWAY.

Dag Hammarskjöld

WHEN YOUR DREAMS TURN TO DUST, VACUUM.

Desmond Tutu

EXPERIENCE IS WHAT YOU GET WHEN YOU DON'T GET WHAT YOU WANT.

Dan Stanford

LIFE IS SIMPLE, IT'S JUST NOT EASY.

Anonymous

LEARN FROM YESTERDAY, LIVE FOR TODAY, HOPE FOR TOMORROW. THE IMPORTANT THING IS NOT TO STOP QUESTIONING.

Albert Einstein

DO WHAT
YOU CAN,
WITH WHAT
YOU HAVE,
WHERE
YOU ARE.

Theodore Roosevelt

LIFE IS JUST ONE DAMNED THING AFTER ANOTHER.

Elbert Hubbard

IN THREE
WORDS I
CAN SUM UP
EVERYTHING
I'VE
LEARNED
ABOUT LIFE:
IT GOES ON.

Robert Frost

LIFE ISN'T ABOUT
WAITING FOR
THE STORM
TO PASS; IT'S
ABOUT LEARNING
TO DANCE IN
THE RAIN.

Anonymous

WITHOUT SOME GOAL AND SOME EFFORT TO REACH IT, NO ONE CAN LIVE.

Fyodor Dostoyevsky

WHEN I HEAR
SOMEBODY
SIGH, 'LIFE
IS HARD,' I
AM ALWAYS
TEMPTED
TO ASK,
'COMPARED
TO WHAT?'

Sydney J. Harris

I HAVE SOMETIMES
BEEN WILDLY,
DESPAIRINGLY,
ACUTELY
MISERABLE... BUT
THROUGH IT ALL
I STILL KNOW...
TO BE ALIVE IS A
GRAND THING.

Agatha Christie

WHAT DO WE LIVE FOR, IF IT IS NOT TO MAKE LIFE LESS DIFFICULT FOR EACH OTHER?

George Eliot

LIFE ISN'T
ABOUT FINDING
YOURSELF. LIFE IS
ABOUT CREATING
YOURSELF.

George Bernard Shaw

IF MY
DOCTOR
TOLD ME I
HAD ONLY
SIX MINUTES
TO LIVE,
I WOULDN'T
BROOD.
I'D TYPE
A LITTLE
FASTER.

Isaac Asimov

OUR EYES
NEED TO BE
WASHED BY
OUR TEARS...
SO THAT WE
CAN SEE
LIFE WITH A
CLEARER VIEW
AGAIN.

Alex Tan

LOOK AT LIFE THROUGH THE WINDSHIELD, NOT THE REAR-VIEW MIRROR.

Byrd Baggett

OBSTACLES
ARE THOSE
FRIGHTFUL
THINGS YOU
SEE WHEN
YOU TAKE
YOUR EYES
OFF THE
GOAL.

Henry Ford

THE STEEPER
THE MOUNTAIN,
THE HARDER
THE CLIMB, THE
BETTER THE
VIEW FROM THE
FINISHING LINE.

Anonymous

WHEN YOU COME TO A ROADBLOCK, TAKE A DETOUR.

Mary Kay Ash

IT'S JUST LIFE. JUST LIVE IT.

Terri Guillemets

DON'T GET YOUR
KNICKERS IN A
KNOT. NOTHING
IS SOLVED AND IT
JUST MAKES YOU
WALK FUNNY.

Kathryn Carpenter

BAD TIMES HAVE A SCIENTIFIC VALUE. THESE ARE OCCASIONS A GOOD LEARNER WOULD NOT MISS.

Ralph Waldo Emerson

IF YOU'RE
ALREADY WALKING
ON THIN ICE, YOU
MIGHT AS WELL
DANCE.

Proverb

WHEN ASKED IF MY CUP IS HALF-FULL OR HALF-EMPTY MY ONLY RESPONSE IS THAT I AM THANKFUL I HAVE A CUP.

Sam Lefkowitz

ONE DOESN'T
DISCOVER
NEW LANDS
WITHOUT
CONSENTING
TO LOSE
SIGHT OF
THE SHORE
FOR A VERY
LONG TIME.

André Gide

MY GRANDFATHER ALWAYS SAID THAT LIVING IS LIKE LICKING HONEY OFF A THORN.

Louis Adamic

I ASK
NOT FOR
A LIGHTER
BURDEN,
BUT FOR
BROADER
SHOULDERS.

Jewish proverb

THE BEST WAY
OUT IS ALWAYS
THROUGH.

Robert Frost

IT JUST WOULDN'T BE A PICNIC WITHOUT THE ANTS.

Anonymous

WHEN IT IS DARKEST, MEN SEE THE STARS.

Ralph Waldo Emerson

SMOOTH SEAS DO NOT MAKE SKILFUL SAILORS.

African proverb

THE DARKEST HOUR HAS ONLY SIXTY MINUTES.

Morris Mandel

THE AVERAGE
PENCIL IS SEVEN
INCHES LONG,
WITH JUST A HALF-
INCH ERASER
- IN CASE YOU
THOUGHT OPTIMISM
WAS DEAD.

Robert Brault

IT IS NOT THE MOMENT WE CONQUER BUT OURSELVES.

Edmund Hillary

I TRY TO TAKE ONE DAY AT A TIME, BUT SOMETIMES SEVERAL DAYS ATTACK ME AT ONCE.

Jennifer Yane

THE ROAD TO SUCCESS IS DOTTED WITH MANY TEMPTING PARKING PLACES.

Anonymous

IF AT FIRST
YOU DON'T
SUCCEED,
FIND OUT
IF THE
LOSER GETS
ANYTHING.

Bill Lyon

WHEN YOU
COME TO THE END
OF YOUR ROPE,
TIE A KNOT AND
HANG ON.

Franklin D. Roosevelt

EVEN IF YOU FALL ON YOUR FACE, YOU'RE STILL MOVING FORWARD.

Robert Gallagher

EVERYTHING
IS OK IN
THE END.
IF IT'S NOT
OK, THEN
IT'S NOT
THE END.

Anonymous

**EVER TRIED.
EVER FAILED.
NO MATTER.
TRY AGAIN.
FAIL AGAIN.
FAIL BETTER.**

Samuel Beckett

WHEN LIFE TAKES THE WIND OUT OF YOUR SAILS, IT IS TO TEST YOU AT THE OARS.

Robert Brault

SINCE THE HOUSE
IS ON FIRE LET US
WARM OURSELVES.

Italian proverb

WATER WHICH IS TOO PURE HAS NO FISH.

Ts'ai Ken T'an

SHOOT FOR
THE MOON.
EVEN IF
YOU MISS,
YOU'LL LAND
AMONG THE
STARS.

Les Brown

I QUIT
BEING AFRAID
WHEN MY FIRST
VENTURE FAILED
AND THE SKY
DIDN'T FALL
DOWN.

Allen H. Neuharth

THE SEASON OF FAILURE IS THE BEST TIME FOR SOWING THE SEEDS OF SUCCESS.

Paramahansa Yogananda

NO ONE EVER
WON A CHESS
GAME BY BETTING
ON EACH MOVE.
SOMETIMES YOU
HAVE TO MOVE
BACKWARD TO GET
A STEP FORWARD.

Amar Gopal Bose

THE TROUBLE WITH DOING SOMETHING RIGHT THE FIRST TIME IS THAT NOBODY APPRECIATES HOW DIFFICULT IT WAS.

Walt West

I DON'T' HAVE
PET PEEVES LIKE
SOME PEOPLE.
I HAVE WHOLE
KENNELS OF
IRRITATION.

Whoopi Goldberg

I HAVE LOVE IN
ME THE LIKES OF
WHICH YOU CAN
SCARCELY IMAGINE
AND RAGE THE
LIKES OF WHICH
YOU WOULD NOT
BELIEVE. IF I
CANNOT SATISFY
THE ONE, I WILL
INDULGE THE
OTHER.

Mary Shelley

HE WHO HAS A WHY TO LIVE CAN BEAR ALMOST ANY HOW.

Friedrich Nietzsche

NEVER BE
AFRAID TO TRY
SOMETHING NEW.
REMEMBER,
AMATEURS
BUILT THE ARK.
PROFESSIONALS
BUILT THE *TITANIC*.

Anonymous

THE TROUBLE WITH THE FUTURE IS THAT IT USUALLY ARRIVES BEFORE WE'RE READY FOR IT.

Arnold H. Glasow

THIS LIFE IS NOT FOR COMPLAINT, BUT FOR SATISFACTION.

Henry David Thoreau

DO NOT BE ANXIOUS ABOUT TOMORROW, FOR TOMORROW WILL BE ANXIOUS FOR ITSELF. LET THE DAY'S OWN TROUBLE BE SUFFICIENT FOR THE DAY.

Matthew 6:34

A MAN'S LIFE IS INTERESTING PRIMARILY WHEN HE HAS FAILED.

Georges Clemenceau

ANGER IS A
GREAT FORCE. IF
YOU CONTROL
IT, IT CAN BE
TRANSMUTED INTO
A POWER WHICH
CAN MOVE THE
WHOLE WORLD.

William Shenstone

YOU CAN'T TURN BACK THE CLOCK BUT YOU CAN WIND IT UP AGAIN.

Bonnie Prudden

WHEN YOU ARISE
IN THE MORNING,
THINK OF WHAT
A PRECIOUS
PRIVILEGE IT IS
TO BE ALIVE -
TO BREATHE, TO
THINK, TO ENJOY
AND TO LOVE.

Marcus Aurelius

FAILURES ARE LIKE SKINNED KNEES: PAINFUL BUT SUPERFICIAL.

Ross Perot

ONCE THE
GAME IS
OVER, THE
KING AND
THE PAWN
GO BACK
INTO THE
SAME BOX.

Latin proverb

BIRDS SING AFTER
A STORM. WHY
SHOULDN'T WE?

Rose Fitzgerald Kennedy

THERE HAS BEEN MUCH TRAGEDY IN MY LIFE; AT LEAST HALF OF IT ACTUALLY HAPPENED.

Mark Twain

FLOWERS
GROW OUT
OF DARK
MOMENTS.

Corita Kent

**TURN
DIFFICULTIES
INTO LEARNING
OPPORTUNITIES.**

Albert Einstein

SUCCESS
AND
FAILURE ARE
GREATLY
OVERRATED.
BUT FAILURE
GIVES YOU A
WHOLE LOT
MORE TO
TALK ABOUT.

Hildegard Knef

YOU CAN'T HAVE
EVERYTHING...
WHERE WOULD
YOU PUT IT?

Steven Wright

ADVERSITY HAS EVER BEEN CONSIDERED THE STATE IN WHICH A MAN MOST EASILY BECOMES ACQUAINTED WITH HIMSELF.

Samuel Johnson

IF YOU ARE
IRRITATED
BY EVERY
RUB, HOW
WILL YOUR
MIRROR BE
POLISHED?

Rumi

RULE NUMBER ONE IS, DON'T SWEAT THE SMALL STUFF. RULE NUMBER TWO IS, IT'S ALL SMALL STUFF.

Robert Eliot

IF THERE
MUST BE
TROUBLE,
LET IT BE
IN MY DAY,
THAT MY
CHILD MAY
HAVE PEACE.

Thomas Paine

WHEN LIFE LOOKS
LIKE IT'S FALLING
APART, IT MAY
JUST BE FALLING
IN PLACE.

Beverly Solomon

LIFE IS A SHIPWRECK, BUT WE MUST NOT FORGET TO SING IN THE LIFEBOATS.

Voltaire

IF YOU
DON'T THINK
EVERY DAY
IS A GOOD
DAY, JUST
TRY MISSING
ONE.

Cavett Robert

THE TROUBLE WITH MOST PEOPLE IS THAT THEY THINK WITH THEIR HOPES OR FEARS OR WISHES RATHER THAN WITH THEIR MINDS.

Will Durant

A TRULY HAPPY PERSON IS ONE WHO CAN ENJOY THE SCENERY WHILE ON A DETOUR.

Anonymous

SOMETIMES
LIFE'S HELL. BUT
HEY! WHATEVER
GETS THE
MARSHMALLOWS
TOASTY.

J. Andrew Helt

THERE ARE TWO WAYS OF MEETING DIFFICULTIES: YOU ALTER THE DIFFICULTIES, OR YOU ALTER YOURSELF TO MEET THEM.

Phyllis Bottome

I CAN'T COMPLAIN, BUT SOMETIMES I STILL DO.

Joe Walsh

I'VE DECIDED
THAT THE STUFF
FALLING THROUGH
THE CRACKS IS
CONFETTI AND I'M
HAVING A PARTY!

Betsy Cañas Garmon

ALWAYS FORGIVE YOUR ENEMIES; NOTHING ANNOYS THEM SO MUCH.

Oscar Wilde

THE NECESSITY OF
THE TIMES, MORE
THAN EVER, CALLS
FOR OUR UTMOST
CIRCUMSPECTION,
DELIBERATION,
FORTITUDE, AND
PERSEVERANCE.

Samuel Adams

ALL THINGS ARE DIFFICULT BEFORE THEY ARE EASY.

Thomas Fuller

THE
GREATER
THE
DIFFICULTY,
THE
GREATER
THE GLORY.

Marcus Tullius Cicero

DIFFICULTIES STRENGTHEN THE MIND, AS LABOUR DOES THE BODY.

Seneca

PERSEVERANCE, DEAR MY LORD, KEEPS HONOUR BRIGHT.

William Shakespeare

OUR GREATEST
GLORY IS NOT IN
NEVER FALLING,
BUT IN RISING
EVERY TIME
WE FALL.

Confucius

A PROBLEM IS A CHANCE FOR YOU TO DO YOUR BEST.

Duke Ellington

CONSIDER THE POSTAGE STAMP. IT SECURES SUCCESS THROUGH ITS ABILITY TO STICK TO ONE THING TILL IT GETS THERE.

Josh Billings

THE ELEVATOR TO SUCCESS IS OUT OF ORDER. YOU'LL HAVE TO USE THE STAIRS... ONE STEP AT A TIME.

Joe Girard

A DOSE OF ADVERSITY IS OFTEN AS NEEDFUL AS A DOSE OF MEDICINE.

Proverb

THE PAST IS A
GUIDEPOST, NOT A
HITCHING POST.

L. Thomas Holdcroft

A GEM CANNOT BE POLISHED WITHOUT FRICTION, NOR A MAN PERFECTED WITHOUT TRIALS.

Chinese proverb

THE
DIFFERENCE
BETWEEN
STUMBLING
BLOCKS AND
STEPPING
STONES IS
HOW YOU
USE THEM.

Anonymous

I HAVE WOVEN A PARACHUTE OUT OF EVERYTHING BROKEN.

William Stafford

COURAGE IS GOING FROM FAILURE TO FAILURE WITHOUT LOSING ENTHUSIASM.

Winston Churchill

THE LIFE OF MAN
IS A JOURNEY; A
JOURNEY THAT MUST
BE TRAVELLED,
HOWEVER BAD THE
ROADS OR THE
ACCOMMODATION.

Oliver Goldsmith

ALL OF US COULD TAKE A LESSON FROM THE WEATHER; IT PAYS NO ATTENTION TO CRITICISM.

Anonymous

YOU MISS ONE
HUNDRED
PER CENT OF
THE SHOTS
YOU DON'T
TAKE.

Wayne Gretzky

NOBODY SAYS
YOU MUST LAUGH,
BUT A SENSE
OF HUMOUR
CAN HELP YOU
OVERLOOK THE
UNATTRACTIVE...
AND SMILE
THROUGH THE DAY.

Ann Landers

SCAR TISSUE IS STRONGER THAN REGULAR TISSUE. REALISE THE STRENGTH, MOVE ON.

Henry Rollins

LIFE APPEARS TO
ME TOO SHORT
TO BE SPENT
IN NURSING
ANIMOSITY, OR
REGISTERING
WRONGS.

Charlotte Brontë

IF YOUR SHIP DOESN'T COME IN, SWIM OUT TO IT.

Jonathan Winters

I HAVE A
SIMPLE
PHILOSOPHY:
FILL WHAT'S
EMPTY; EMPTY
WHAT'S FULL;
SCRATCH
WHERE IT
ITCHES.

Alice Roosevelt Longworth

YOUR LIFE IS AN OCCASION. RISE TO IT.

Suzanne Weyn

THE HARDER YOU FALL, THE HIGHER YOU BOUNCE.

Doug Horton

AFTER A YEAR
IN THERAPY, MY
PSYCHIATRIST SAID
TO ME, 'MAYBE
LIFE ISN'T FOR
EVERYONE.'

Larry Brown

LIFE IS 'TRYING THINGS TO SEE IF THEY WORK'.

Ray Bradbury

MAKE
THE MOST
OF YOUR
REGRETS...
TO REGRET
DEEPLY IS TO
LIVE AFRESH.

Henry David Thoreau

I'VE LEARNED THAT WHEN YOU HARBOUR BITTERNESS, HAPPINESS WILL DOCK ELSEWHERE.

Andy Rooney

IT HAS
BEEN MY
PHILOSOPHY
OF LIFE
THAT
DIFFICULTIES
VANISH
WHEN FACED
BOLDLY.

Isaac Asimov

I TAKE A SIMPLE
VIEW OF LIFE:
KEEP YOUR EYES
OPEN AND GET ON
WITH IT.

Laurence Olivier

THINK OF ALL THE BEAUTY STILL LEFT AROUND YOU AND BE HAPPY.

Anne Frank

FAILURE IS
ONLY THE
OPPORTUNITY
TO BEGIN
AGAIN,
ONLY THIS
TIME MORE
WISELY.

Henry Ford

TURN YOUR FACE TO THE SUN AND THE SHADOWS FALL BEHIND YOU.

Maori proverb

ONE OF THE BEST LESSONS YOU CAN LEARN IN LIFE IS TO MASTER HOW TO REMAIN CALM.

Catherine Pulsifer

YOU CAN'T MAKE
AN OMELETTE
WITHOUT
BREAKING EGGS.

Proverb

NEVER, NEVER, NEVER GIVE UP.

Winston Churchill

BE COMFORTABLE
BEING
UNCOMFORTABLE.
IT MAY GET
TOUGH, BUT IT'S
A SMALL PRICE
TO PAY FOR
LIVING A DREAM.

Peter McWilliams

EXPERIENCE: THAT MOST BRUTAL OF TEACHERS.

C. S. Lewis

THE SCORE NEVER INTERESTED ME, ONLY THE GAME.

Mae West

TOUGH
TIMES NEVER
LAST. TOUGH
PEOPLE DO.

Robert Schuller

THIS TOO SHALL PASS.

Anonymous

THINGS
TURN OUT
BEST FOR
THE PEOPLE
WHO MAKE
THE BEST
OF THE WAY
THINGS
TURN OUT.

John Wooden